A Visit to the Fire Station

by Rosalyn Clark

BUMBA BOOKS™

LERNER PUBLICATIONS ◆ MINNEAPOLIS

Note to Educators:

Throughout this book, you'll find critical thinking questions. These can be used to engage young readers in thinking critically about the topic and in using the text and photos to do so.

Lerner Publications Company
A division of Lerner Publishing Group, Inc.
241 First Avenue North
Minneapolis, MN 55401 USA

For reading levels and more information, look up this title at www.lernerbooks.com.

Library of Congress Cataloging-in-Publication Data

Names: Clark, Rosalyn, 1990– author.
Title: A visit to the fire station / by Rosalyn Clark.
Description: Minneapolis : Lerner Publications, [2018] | Series: Bumba books. Places we go | Audience: Age 4–7. | Audience: K to Grade 3. | Includes bibliographical references and index.
Identifiers: LCCN 2016046972 (print) | LCCN 2016052453 (ebook) | ISBN 9781512433722 (lb : alk. paper) | ISBN 9781512455618 (pb : alk. paper) | ISBN 9781512450439 (eb pdf)
Subjects: LCSH: Fire extinction—Juvenile literature. | Fire stations—Juvenile literature.
Classification: LCC TH9148 .C55 2018 (print) | LCC TH9148 (ebook) | DDC 363.37—dc23

LC record available at https://lccn.loc.gov/2016046972

Manufactured in the United States of America
1—CG—7/15/17

Table of Contents

Time for a Field Trip

It is time for a class field trip!

We are visiting a fire station.

FIRE DEPARTMENT
FIRE DEPT.

We meet a firefighter.

She shows us around

the station.

We see suits and helmets.

Suits protect firefighters from fire.

Helmets protect them from

falling objects.

What might

fall in a burning

building?

23

We see fire trucks

and fire engines.

They have sirens.

The firefighter turns

on a siren.

It is loud!

Why do you think fire trucks and engines have sirens and lights?

"STILL STANDING"
www.nyc.gov.fdny
CITY OF NEW YORK
F.D.
N.Y.
FERRARA
10
BRAVERY

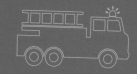

Fire trucks have ladders.

Firefighters climb ladders

to reach fires.

Fire engines have hoses.

Hoses spray water.

Water puts out fires.

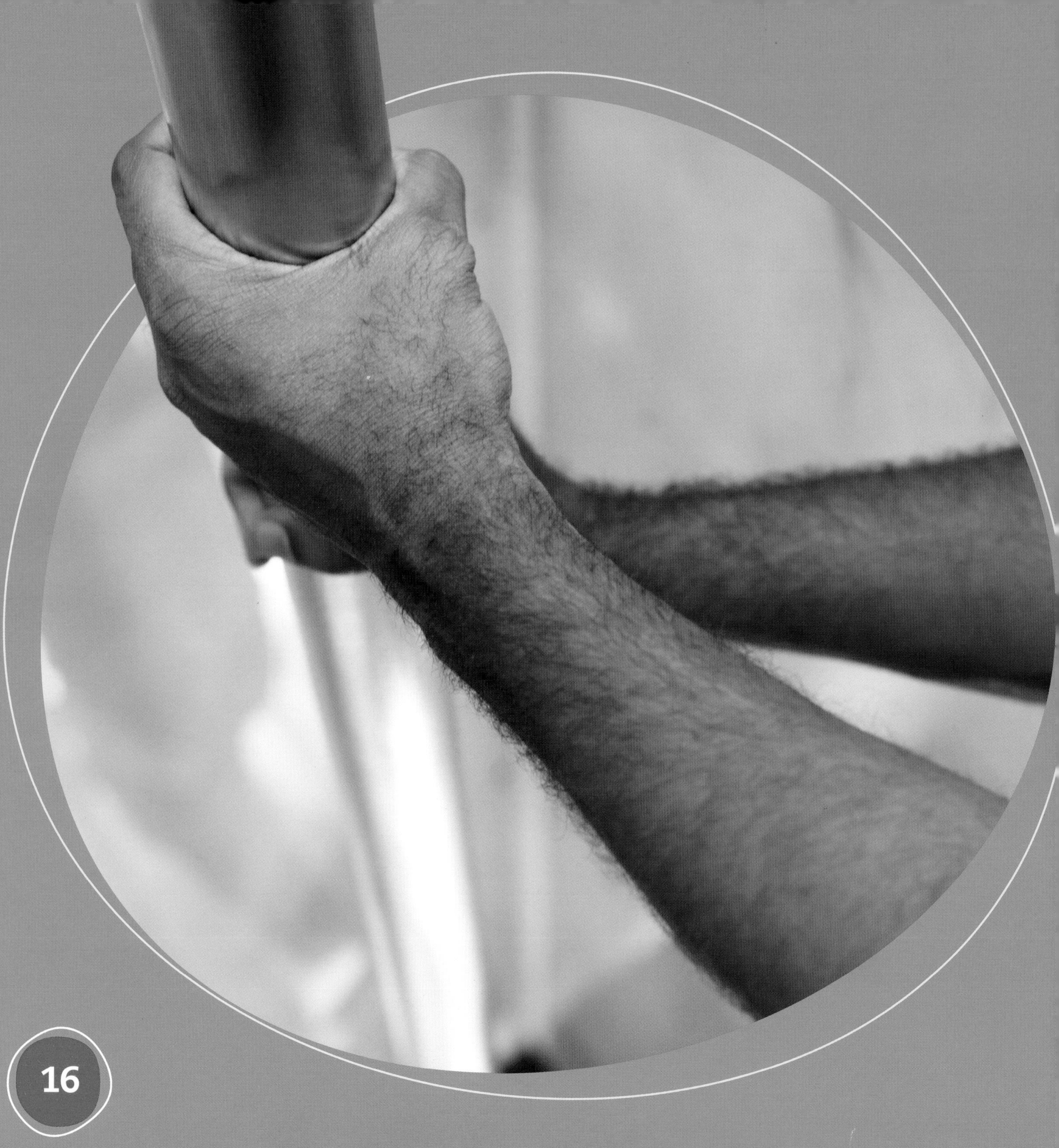

Firefighters need to get to the fire fast.

The fire station has a pole.

Firefighters slide down the pole.

Why do firefighters need to get to fires fast?

Firefighters work hard.

The fire station has

a kitchen.

Firefighters eat and

relax there.

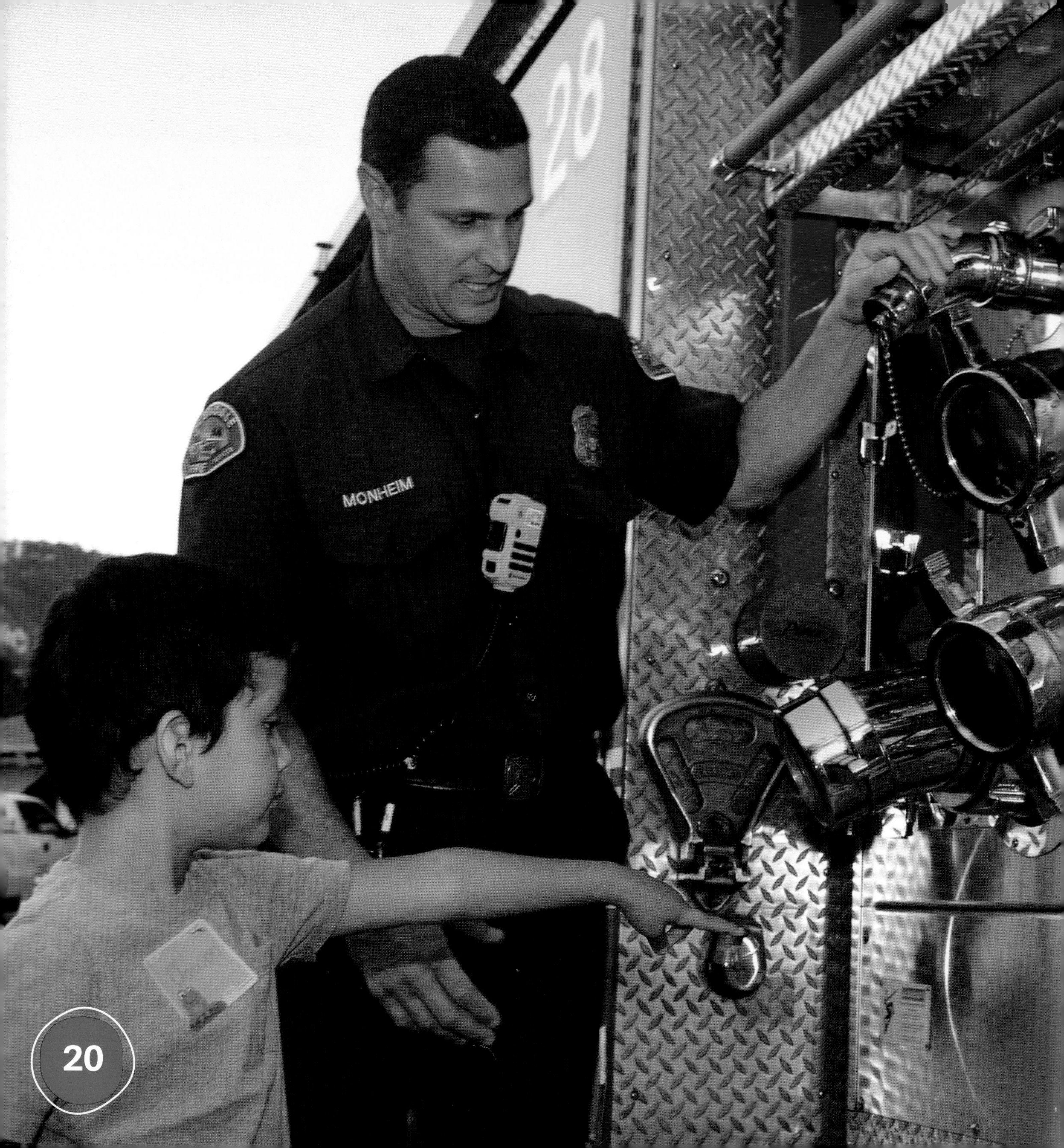
28
MONHEIM

Fire stations have everything
a firefighter needs.
Would you like to visit a fire station?

What to See at a Fire Station

Picture Glossary

firefighter

someone who works to put out fires

protect

to keep something or someone safe

relax

to spend time resting after working hard

sirens

devices that make loud sounds

Read More

Anderson, Sheila. *Fire Station.* Minneapolis: LernerClassroom, 2008.

Miller, Connie Colwell. *I'll Be a Firefighter.* Mankato, MN: Amicus Illustrated Riverstream, 2017.

Silverman, Buffy. *How Do Fire Trucks Work?* Minneapolis: Lerner Publications, 2016.

Index

Photo Credits

The images of this book are used with the permission of: © AlexSava/iStock.com, p. 5; © Micah Youello/iStock.com, pp. 6–7; © Jerry Sharp/Shutterstock.com, pp. 9, 23 (top right); © Lukas Maverick Greyson/Shutterstock.com, pp. 10–11, 23 (bottom right); © potowizard/Shutterstock.com, pp. 12, 23 (top left); © Dave Logan/iStock.com, pp. 14–15; © Monkey Business Images/Shutterstock.com, pp. 16, 18–19, 23 (bottom left); © Dan Holm/Shutterstock.com, p. 20; © Le Do/Shutterstock.com, p. 22 (left); © skodonnell/iStock.com, p. 22 (right).

Front Cover: © Chris Rogers/Thinkstock.com.